Dialogues

of the

Silent Mind

Subtle conversations
with the Self in the form of
rhythmic & unexpected Quatrains

Jim Ryan

ISBN: 978-0-9935350-4-8
Eternal Point Publishers
Cover Design by
Pixel Studios

For Worldwide Distribution

INTRODUCTION

Understanding and awareness, two close companions and two main goals for the spiritual traveller; and as we try to grasp and hold and assimilate what we believe are long sought-after truths, we discover both these to be very elusive and mercurial.

Experiencing new awareness can be described as like coming out from a long, dark tunnel and suddenly there's blinding white light, with all its glare and brightness. At that moment, there is just the experience of light and so too, on our spiritual journey, having been so long deprived of understanding, now connecting with a new awareness, a new light, a new understanding, we feel that we have found, we have arrived. Yet, as we gradually get used to the light, to the new effect, it soon becomes evident that the light is only a consequence and an experience of the forms of that new awareness.

As we begin to re-adjust to these new experiences and new avenues of understanding, consciousness starts to awaken and begins to attempt to discern and clarify what was formerly known and unknown, and place this new understanding into what it perceives to be the right form and nature of things.

Yet, this 'knowing' will almost invariably be illusory, for as the saying goes, "we see things as we are, not as they are." For consciousness is truly a chameleon in nature, being like an evolving multi-faceted sphere of component understandings, ever changing, reformulating, synthesizing and moving towards its ultimate state of being.

Our journey is one of search and discovery; yet, even when we reach those eureka moments of realisation, the journey, our awakening, still continues; for truth comes often to us like new-found clay that we then have to refine and reshape to reveal its deep and real form. So we place it on the potter's wheel of awareness and, as we continually turn it, we need to observe it and, with each turn and observation, it changes. Yet, still not touching or holding, for it is still formulating, otherwise it will crumple and be lost.

I am still watching, trying to learn, connect and make greater meaning of what I know.

Dialogues

1

I am like the wind,
Free and flowing,
Gently brushing and touching,
Awakening those who have not noticed the
sun.

2

I am like a feather,
Weightless, light and soft,
Separated and free,
Able to hold, to ride, the wind of changing
circumstance.

3

I am like the sand,
Receptive and supportive,
Malleable to each new and accepted step,
But leaving no trail, so each one can discover
their own path

4

I am like a blade of grass,
One amongst so many,
I am separate and the same,
Yet, still a unique strand in the matrix of
consciousness.

5

I am like an orange.
In my innermost state,
I am sweet and full of goodness,
So I peel back my mask and reveal myself.

6

I am like water,
Transparent and clear,
Refreshing, reviving the thirsty, the dying,
Returning, recycling and renewing the world.

7

I am like death,
I let go of what was held,
Closing the door on my fears and my sorrows
and old sad memory,
Allowing then the laughing, dancing child to
come and sing her song.

8

I am held firm in God's vision,
Where can I go?
Where can I escape or turn,
So I must stay.

9

I am not my many masks,
And not the things that are not my masks,
I am like everything, but not like any of them,
I am just uniquely me.

10

I am subtle and light,
Framed by the effects of my interactive life,
Creating a story, a picture,
But this tells a lie.

11

I am like a spoon,
I blend the ingredients,
Of each one's speciality,
And I then go and drink that medicine.

12

I am like a cloud,
Often full of negative thoughts,
So denying myself a clear and open sky.
Yet, in letting them go, I discover a new and
different landscape.

13

I am happy and free,
Because I have given away
All my concerns and worries and
responsibilities
Directly to God.

14

I am like a radio,
Tuned to the frequency of silence.
Hearing now the songs of God,
I now dance the dance of truth.

15

I am like a fence,
I divide and separate,
Keeping things in sections and compartments,
Yet, I have a gate that opens to all.

16

I am like a path,
Crossed by many paths,
Going here and there,
But only my path can take me where I have to
go.

17

I am like the sun,
Whose light is often shielded by cloud and
darkness.
Yet, all things pass,
And I still shall remain a shining light.

18

I am like a sink,
Choosing to either,
Hold and use that which comes,
Or allow those things to just flow on through.

19

I am like an iron,
Pushing and pressing,
Trying to resolve and straighten things out,
But occasionally forgetting to turn on the
switch.

20

I am sweetness and light,
Changing bitterness and anger and old ways
of grief,
Into light feelings and laughter and new ways
of seeing,
But aware that too much creates overload and
pain or even death.

21

I am complete and content,
I have no need to search, to call out,
I have what I need,
For I am what I previously looked for.

22

I am like a mirror,
I have no mask,
No parading image.
By remaining clear, I allow others to see their
truth.

23

I am like a mother,
Giving birth to thoughts and ideas,
And as a trustee I have no attachments,
So I share and let things go.

24

I am like a tree,
Full of beauty and attainment,
I cannot keep and hold these things,
For all things change, so I share them now.

25

I am like a bird,
Whose song is heard,
But is quickly lost
To the blowing wind.

26

I am like a nail on the finger
Of the hand of the body
Which is truth,
So my only responsibility is to stay clean.

27

I am like a matchstick,
Striking the box of spiritual memory,
I light the flame of awareness
And the fire of original love.

28

I am like a field.
The thoughts I sow,
Yield either flowers of subtle fragrance
Or weeds of thorny brambles.

29

I am a pupil in the eye of God,
Who studies the I
To know the I,
So that I then can finish the I.

30

I am like a snake,
In shedding my ego skin of old opinion
I also relinquish all past natures,
And I move closer to who I really am.

31

I am moving towards my final scenes,
And on the opposite side in the opposite way,
Others pass by,
Lost and unaware.

32

I am like a ploughed field,
Where the flowers and fruits have now gone,
Allowing the seeds of new awareness to be
planted,
And a new growth to come again and bloom.

33

I am walking with you,
Seeing and hearing the things you do and say,
Yet, I do not hold and engage with them,
For I am with the One.

34

I am like the rain,
Refreshing and restoring,
And when I have done,
I will come again in the cycle of return.

35

I am like a tree,
Rooted in self-awareness.
Silently I reach out to embrace the light.
What else do I need to do?

36

I am somewhere else,
Yet, you and others believe otherwise,
These words testify to a location,
But I know differently.

37

I am looking at you,
But I only see myself,
I see and hear what you do and say,
And I think, what is it that I have to change?

38

I am looking at God.
In saying this, are you seeing the same?
If so, others in turn,
Will also know the One.

39

I am one with myself,
I am one with others,
I am one with God.
Are you wondering, why you are not
experiencing the same?

40

I am like a flapping bird
Who flies against the wind,
Until I realise,
I need to stop and change direction.

41

I am remembering God,
The one whom all used to know.
Yet now, most, in their confusion,
Only remember themselves.

42

I am like the silence of the trees,
The stillness of the land,
The beauty of the setting sun,
And, unfortunately, like the impetuousness of
the incoming tide.

43

I am on a battlefield,
Where everyone is slain,
So I study to stay alive
In order that I, too, may die.

44

I am a celestial being,
A light being,
A subtle being,
Who enjoys a cup of tea.

45

I am awake,
Yet, in the steamy mirror of awareness,
I struggle to see myself, as one form clouds
another,
Until I realise that I need to stop looking.

46

I am trying to help myself,
I am trying to help others,
I am trying to solve many problems,
Until I realise that I'm not God.

47

I am gradually letting go of the illusory world,
And the things I cling to are slowly slipping
away,
So now my arms are becoming freed
For me to embrace the spiritual Father.

48

I am focused on myself,
On what I need to do,
On my thoughts and attitudes, not on you and
your concerns,
But you still have my love.

49

I am like a boat,
Travelling through the waves of awareness,
While others, watching,
Wish that they too were also a travelling boat.

50

I am content,
No longer asking or demanding.
For, centred in my original, spiritual nature,
I enable others to receive the experience of
contentment.

51

I am amazed,
At the infinite variety of life.
At times, I feel small and inconsequential,
Yet, in God's eyes, significant and relevant.

52

I am crossing the field of action,
Tired, used and long abused,
But now not stopping, just travelling through,
For I have done my time.

53

I am like the natural worlds,
Growing, unfolding and declining,
And, like the turning cycle,
I will also begin it all again.

54

I am filling and full,
I am travelling and have arrived,
I am where I am supposed to be,
Yet, I know I should be somewhere else.

55

I am attracted by your attraction,
Yet, in this shimmer of illusion,
Comes a reminder, an image of whom I am,
So I let your attraction pass.

56

I am holding God's hand,
He is holding my hand,
And we are dancing, and you can join us,
But you first must give your hand.

57

I am helping the hurt
And pain of others,
By considering their sorrow to be my sorrow,
And sending them good wishes and healing
feelings of love.

58

I am remembering my form of love and truth,
Holding on to the One who is the truth,
So my words, though maybe not so carefully
constructed,
Yet, contain the breath and energy of the
Supreme.

59

I am opening to my beauty,
Each step reveals my form,
I am opening to my power,
My life reveals my love.

60

I am like a caterpillar,
Devouring the food of knowledge.
I am like a chrysalis, cocooned in the centre of
silence.
I am like a butterfly, flower-focussed and free.

61

I am a conduit for God's great light,
A diamond,
Refracting the rays of spiritual power,
Into the heart receptors of the world.

62

I am none of my many projected forms,
None of my numerous beliefs and assembled
concepts.
I am without image,
Just light, energy and love.

63

I am involved in three great tasks,
Forgiving myself and forgiving others,
Accepting what has happened and what is
happening,
And staying in the present with who I am.

64

I am taking the medicine of happiness,
A concoction of self-awareness,
Spiritual relationships and the position of a
detached observer.
A medicine that finishes all suffering.

65

I am giving all my rubbish to God,
I have no strength any more,
He can take all my burdens and worries,
He is big enough.

66

I am now edging into the unlimited,
The shoreline of the limited world is fast
fading,
Fears, worries and the questioning mind are
flickering and finishing,
And I am smiling.

67

I am like the ocean,
My surface world, each thought, each word,
now a wave of love,
And in the deep, in the depths of my silent
self,
I gather power and watch the game.

68

I am at peace,
Having now discarded my old false face and
public image,
That pushed, pointed and picked at every part
and unfolding scene,
Now content, knowing all is as it should be.

69

I am no longer holding onto the illusions of
the material world,
Which stand, shake, fall and then disappear,
I sit separate,
Supported by the subtle light of God.

70

I am sitting at the edge of time,
But I have little difficulty
In turning away from the chaos of the
collapsing worlds,
As I face the new and forming day.

71

I am no longer shouting at the world,
For I have stepped away
Into the still, silent lands,
And I have become very quiet.

72

I am no longer gazing in the mirror,
No longer courting the fame of others,
No longer attracted by your face,
For now I just sing God's praise.

73

I am signing for the new age,
A new contract for a new life,
Old thoughts, nature and attitudes are
stopped,
As I take up on the blueprint of the document
of truth.

74

I am like a bird
Sitting at the top of a tree,
Which below is crumbling and decaying.
Yet, I am ready to fly, seeing a new tree just
ahead.

75

I am like a wood
Containing many paths and pathways
And only I can walk them.
If you should try, you surely will get lost.

76

I am flowing in the energy matrix of
consciousness,
Each thought and emotion changes my form
and my direction,
So with these I am cautious and careful,
Learning just to observe and appreciate the
patterned harmony of life.

77

I am happy with who I am,
Able then to be content
With you and your world.
Linking in this love, we create a family.

78

I am hearing and seeing you,
I smile and nod as you relate your world,
But it is not mine,
Mine is another place.

79

I am like a clock,
Though timeless and eternal,
I am caught in time,
Yearning for the freedom of another time.

80

I am like a dancer who has danced with many,
We came together, danced and now they
dance elsewhere,
So I let them go with love and good wishes,
And I, in happiness, now dance with God.

81

I am no longer living in the shadow lands of
the old world,
That distorts, fragments and replicates old
fears.
Now, with God's support,
I face, challenge and change the illusions of
the dark.

82

I am able and capable,
I am patient and peaceful,
I am light and happy and content,
Aren't you?

83

I am like a lamp,
Shining in the darkness,
It shows me my way,
And a way for you to know your way.

84

I am forgetting and remembering,
Not holding your words and acts of the past,
But assimilating your goodness
And reframing it, as part of my part.

85

I am seeing your specialness,
Your efforts to be true,
I step over your shadows and old failed
forms,
And run with you towards the light.

86

I am wishing the world to change and
transform,
I am seeing the chaos, the injustice, the
absence of values,
I shout, I call, I sing out loud.
Until I realise that it's my part that I need to
change.

87

I am an open door to your present needs.
What is it that you have come for?
What is it that I have to give?
So I ensure my hands are always full.

88

I am listening and watching your special
dance,
Yet, in me there is a reaction, no full
acceptance and embrace,
For my ego shadow self shouts, "But look at
me!"
And so I turn and kill it, using your love.

89

I am like a conductor,
Orchestrating my attitudes, feelings and
emotions,
To produce a harmony, a symphony,
Of emerging, cascading love.

90

I am like a pencil,
I note down your goodness,
I draw a line under the past and put a full stop
to old thinking,
And when worn down, I repair to God.

91

I am like the air,
Soft and light and free,
Gently flowing and caressing the fevered
brow,
Reviving the fallen and overturning the
images of false belief.

92

I am walking my path,
It's taking me where I have to go,
So ignore it, turn your back to it,
For your path goes somewhere else.

93

I am finishing and relinquishing all ties with
the restrictive world,
Extricating from the mundane and non-
essential,
Allowing my attitude, vision and creative
thinking
To connect with the field of the unlimited.

94

I am like you,
Questioning and complaining, contrasting and
rejecting,
Not happy, not helping.
Shall we stop?

95

I am aware (so God must be also) of your
pain,
And so the subtle, merciful mind of God
Surely moves, sends vibrations, energies of
supportive love,
To the heart of the crying child.

96

I am content,
Knowing that each scene, each part, is as we
make it,
So I ensure that what I say and do is bound in
spiritual law,
And the result of which is, that I am content.

97

I am recalling what I have attained and
become,
Of the form and nature of who I am,
The relationship I have with the highest One.
So in this strength, gone are my fears and
fluctuating doubts.

98

I am in my light form, soul form, bodiless
state,
Every block, every influence falls away,
The world and its illusions disappear
As I become the fulcrum, the seed of a new
awareness.

99

I am like the gentle, calming seas.
For as the fires of anger bring their flames of
insult and projected pain,
I understand the cause, the effect, of such a
state.
So I step back and allow the breaking waves
of peaceful love to cool the tortured soul.

100

I am giving all to God,
It's an investment,
Yet, though helping me to remove my
sorrows and attachments,
He still has to give me the return.

101

I am like a child,
With no embattled ego, premeditated agendas
and mental cleverness,
I am able to see the fun, the wonder and the
silliness
Of each present moment.

102

I am free of conflict,
For faith in myself, others and in God
Has brought me peace,
So I now no longer shout, demand and
question why.

103

I am like a child, an opening flower,
I have shed the cleverness and stance
Of righteousness and opinion,
Because now I'm small and happy.

104

I am using God's hand of blessing
To help resolve my issues and problems,
For in front of the Great Sun,
I receive solutions to deal with things of
candlelight.

105

I am an incarnation,
Who comes to follow the way of truth,
Who comes to establish the religion, the way
of the spiritual soul,
Who comes centred in God's love, light,
energy.

106

I am a messenger,
Light, empty and detached,
I come with a message,
To be light, empty and detached.

107

I am now able to forget
The accumulated confusions of wrong
thinking,
Because I now take power from God,
And the way becomes clear.

108

I am hidden from you,
For I have drunk the secret elixir of
awareness,
And I know I am who I am.
To be and see the same, you must also drink
the same.

109

I am thinking of the world,
Not with sadness or with sorrow,
But as a mother,
And I hold it in my arms.

110

I am no longer chasing an alluring world,
Which only traps and devours my trusting
heart,
And so turning in silence to the overflowing
Father,
I fill my needs and run no more.

111

I am taking and receiving your grief and your
love,
Yet, my other hand gives it all to God,
Who, receiving it, gives you then the return,
Through blessings of hope, of love and subtle
strength.

112

I am reducing and compacting the world
Of issues and situations and debate,
Refraining from inflating the small and
everyday stuff.
It is a game that we all need to play.

113

I am holding God's love,
It is extraordinary, full of significances,
Naturally maintaining, stabilising, empowering
the mind.
It is this love that does all the work.

114

I am no longer in the shadows, the waiting
rooms of fear,
Not knowing my role, my true and authentic
self.
Now able to recognise the illusions of public
expectation and opinion,
What would monkeys know about the value
of a diamond?

115

I am reminded by the happy, laughing child,
Of what I was and what I am able to be,
And in contrast, my vanities, strivings and
constant fears
Seem ridiculous and utterly pointless.

116

I am now not thinking too much,
Why should I think a lot?
God is now my teacher and drama my guide,
So what do I need to think about?

117

I am telling God everything.
In this dance of repentance, realisation and
forgiveness,
I untangle the past,
Become free and clear, and start to smile
again.

118

I am like the Phoenix,
Igniting the fires of love,
In which all is consumed, finished and
created,
So dying is certainly needed.

119

I am preparing for death,
Letting go of my attachments and labels,
Yet, still maintaining my inner light that is
needed to guide me
Through the dark passageways of a collapsing
world.

120

I am developing love for God,
I am having faith in God's great love,
And this great love gives me faith,
And this faith allows me to experience His
love.

121

I am ever vigilant against the malevolent
assassin of illusion,
Who stalks and seeks to kill my truth.
In identifying him, he is caught,
And with awareness, he is transformed.

122

I am not espousing a religion or a philosophy,
Not advocating the words or books of others,
I am just sharing my experience,
As an inspiration and as a warning.

123

I am seeing and listening and remembering
with my inner heart,
From this seed bed of nurture,
Understanding and awareness
Grows the flower of spiritual love.

124

I am like a stream,
Keeping my form as others join me,
Not stopping, not holding, but negotiating
each obstacle, each aspect,
Till I reach the Ocean, who says, "Ah you've
arrived!"

125

I am seeing with love,
And so what I see changes its form,
And it becomes that which it should be,
And it too becomes the form of love.

126

I am travelling alone, on my own journey.
Your words, advice, directions only delay me.
With smiling tortoise face,
I withdraw; yet, you think I'm dancing.

127

I am trying not to open my hands,
Each step, each scene, offers me plenty.
Yet, only in declining, in closing my inner
door,
Can I truly taste and embrace my highest
truth.

128

I am seeing through many veils,
And each one masks, distorts and deceives my
mind,
So I must pluck, cut and destroy that 'I',
And only then can my heart discern and find
the way.

129

I am like a child,
But I am not seeking approval or acceptance,
For I have no interest or need of your world,
For I am in my own world.

130

I am sharing and expressing my thoughts and
ideas.
You patiently wait for a gap in the traffic,
Then share and express your thoughts and
ideas.
We both smile and nod, thinking only of our
thoughts and ideas.

131

I am love, compassion and joy,
Yet, like a boy with his hands in his pockets,
I struggle to express and share all these,
And so I'm left unsatisfied and discontented.

132

I am changing and evolving,
Becoming something new,
Yet, I have to let it all go,
To change and evolve and become something
new.

133

I am dancing in the world of happiness,
In tune, in step, in time,
Dancing, yet, holding your eyes,
Offering my hand, inviting you also to dance.

134

I am looking at you,
You are doing the same,
Talking and sharing, yet, missing each other,
Now let's dance, become one and finish this
game.

135

I am in silence,
There are no thoughts,
I am separated and freed from old memory,
Now awareness can come.

136

I am seeing attractions, allurements and sights
from the past,
Reviving sorrow's mechanisms and memories
of frequent pain,
So I turn, move and walk away,
Having already discovered their falsehood and
fictitious myths of fulfilment.

137

I am seeing my face in the mirror of my heart,
A face which only I can see,
So I cleanse and clean it of all deception,
For it is the face I show to God.

138

I am like a cloud,
Who draws and fills from the Ocean Father.
In letting go, I bring refreshment and renewal,
And, in becoming empty, I am free again to
fill.

139

I am like a flying bird,
Previously caged in the world of mine,
Held and anchored, tight and secure,
But now opened by spiritual self-awareness.

140

I am using and seeing with my spiritual eye,
I am seeing my brothers, my Father, the cycle
of time,
I am seeing your journey, your opening heart,
I have now finished the spinning of difference
and opinion.

141

I am doing everything for myself,
It is the only world that I can know and
influence,
I am doing everything for you,
For through this I can change my world.

142

I am like the ocean,
Unlimited and boundless, experiencing the
winds of God's refreshment,
In my depths, I find my long forgotten, long
searched-for pearls of spiritual truth,
Given by God for me to wear, for me to
share.

143

I am still trying to change, rearrange the play
of others,
Yet, no-one listens,
And I am left,
Trying to escape this empty cul-de-sac.

144

I am the friend of God,
So I wonder why I wonder
About today, tomorrow and the causes of all
things chaotic,
And not just about the wonder of being
God's friend.

145

I am reminding you about your spiritual
beauty and inner greatness,
When you listen, awareness stirs,
And you receive the power and the courage
To change and finish and move into the light.

146

I am carefully guarding my subtle mind,
Protecting it from illusion's psychopathic
embrace,
Which seeks continually to break
And kill my link with God.

147

I am aware that change and power,
Can only come through God's support,
And only when I let go of my fears, false self-
images and the need for praise,
Then, with awareness, am I able to connect
with His light point presence.

148

I am content and satisfied,
Having found what I sought,
And I know that those who are dissatisfied,
Can only be satisfied through my words,
attitude and satisfaction.

149

I am filled with God's love,
For my heart has heard God's song of the
heart,
Yet, this song of the heart can only be heard
by those with a heart.
For this, first, take back and reclaim your
heart.

150

I am experiencing the effects of the body,
I welcome it's visit,
For it is not an illness.
But the burden of the past becoming light.

151

I am sitting at the fulcrum of two worlds,
On seeing the forms and the games of the
good and not so good,
I become ensnared and trapped,
But seeing the unlimited, I glide into the
world of freedom.

152

I am, through the Father, now a benevolent
being.
For me to be this, it needs others to be non-
benevolent.
It's just a game of influence and mercy,
And later, we switch and play the other's role.

153

I am like a canal,
I flow and follow,
Yet, at times, I wish to wander and break free,
But then what of the others who are to
follow.

154

I am like the autumn leaf,
Which, knowing it is to fall,
Yet, enjoys the beauty and colour of the day,
Then let's go, already anticipating, a new day,
a new dawn, a fresh beginning.

155

I am like a lake,
Clear and still, showing what is real and true,
And so, as I reflect on what I am,
You too then will also see yourself.

156

I am like a boat moving through the seas of
change and fluctuation.
Yet, I give no concern, no focus, to these
matters,
I know things come and things will go,
And I know I have the capacity, the strength,
to keep progressing.

157

I am free of any worries and concerns,
Related to outcomes or success,
For I have long divorced those long-time
companions,
For all responsibilities are now the Father's.

158

I am like the laughing, playful child,
I have no plans, projections or deceitful
malice,
I enjoy and hold the wonder of each present
scene.
Do you, like others, just simply watch?

159

I am like a painting,
Coloured by learning,
Framed by awareness,
Hanging in God's heart.

160

I am deceived when I lack power,
So I check if power is being lost,
Especially through my thoughts,
Which always indicate and inform me how
poorly or how well I'm doing.

161

I am aware that thoughts should be in the
form of concerns,
If not, then I have become careless,
So I need to see and make sure
That this state should be the foremost of my
concerns.

162

I am aware of how close I am to murder.
Each time I hold and accept illusion's hand,
I suppress and attempt to kill my spiritual
intellect,
So I now arrest my attention with warnings
and precautions.

163

I am aware of inner influence, toxins and
poisons,
So I check the diet of my thoughts.
Are they positive, pure and belong to me?
I do this quickly before I lose consciousness.

164

I am sitting in peace, having given up taking,
accumulating, trying for more,
I have stopped obsessing with form and fame
and social acceptance,
I have finished trying to piece the jigsaw of
others' lives.
Now i have time to sit and draw power and
blessings from God.

165

I am like a house builder,
Creating the house of the spiritual world,
I give focus and regard to each part, to each
brick,
And through this, the individual and the
gathering becomes loving, becomes strong.

166

I am closing my eyes and turning my back,
On the defects and weaknesses of others.
Why should I pick up the rubbish
That they are trying to throw away?

167

I am returning all garlands, all flowers of
praise,
A masquerade, a fraud - having done nothing.
Transferring all now to the Father's name,
I receive the soft petals of contentment.

168

I am alert to the dangers, the illusions, of
praise.
Chasing these shadows I soon become empty.
Dancing and bowing and gathering bouquets,
I forget to fill with power,
Leaving me open and vulnerable to the
backwash of old sorrow.

169

I am aware of karmic law, so what you give to
me, I first will give to God,
So you will receive that powerful return.
However, beware, if you give me grief, I will
give that to God as well,
And he might come looking for you, saying,
"Who gave this to me?"

170

I am becoming content and satisfied,
Having stopped the turmoil of why's and
what's and where's,
My mind is free and calm and light,
Enabling me to see others clearly and make
sense of a fast-changing world.

171

I am aware of your lies and defamations,
Yet, I know your heart is of true intention,
For old behaviour and influence often deflects
us.
So dear old friend, let us continue to walk and
dance on the path of love.

172

I am learning about mercy and love.
Yes, it is a support and help for those in
sorrow.
It is also knowing that each one is trying to
shift their weakness
And, in not seeing it, I co-operate, encourage
and help their effort.

173

I am like a house, which previously was
closed, shuttered and dark.
Now, opening up the windows and doors of
my life,
And switching on the light of awareness,
I begin to see things for what they are and
accept myself for who I am.

174

I am digging up what I have hidden,
Too long have I allowed this unconscious,
negative growth to flourish
In those deep, dark corridors of old nature.
Now exposed, they quickly fade and finish.

175

I am opening my eyes,
Free from the fear of deception and
attraction.
Now seeing your journey, your beauty and
your eternal form,
I too, become this, the same as you.

176

I am now free from the chatter of the mind,
Free of the continual waves that question and
confront.
In silence, I now hear your heart,
And I am able to respond.

177

I am alive, having been dead,
I was a corpse, empty and unfeeling.
Yet, through God's magic touch, my soul
stirred and came to life,
And now in this new form, I dance and sing,
"Ah, I am a child again."

178
I am observing my reactions.
My non-embracing heart has no smiles or
inner joy,
I have fallen again into a lightless cave.
Oh ego, your shadow still blocks out the sun!

179
I am now experiencing happiness,
For I have cleared from my awareness the
dead wood of old philosophy.
With realisations opening my heart,
I am able to share my joy.

180
I am quiet and empty of thought.
I create a thought,
I resonate and integrate with its energy,
becoming one.
I am quiet and empty of thought.

181

I am like the ocean,
At the same time, both still and active.
Within, I am calm and peaceful,
And my surface world is sharing, laughing,
refreshing where needed.

182

I am often distracted and drawn to the
glamour and illusions of the path,
So making the destination and task seem long
and difficult.
Yet, remembering the Father, the mirage
dissipates,
And I have again the focus and strength to
carry on.

183

I am hearing fervent philosophies, earnest
answers and points of guidance.
Such sounds though are like the beating of
drums in front of monkeys,
Adding only to the noise of the sorrow-filled
world.
Only silence and the Father of silence can
quieten and heal such troubled hearts.

184

I am light, spiritual energy.
This awareness frees me from old influence,
So becoming open and receptive,
To the support and power of the Supreme.

185

I am centred in the ocean of God's love,
Knowing that every wave will be beneficial,
Healing me, supporting me, empowering me,
Taking me to the place I need to be.

186

I am not clinging or needing to possess.
I have finished those games of attachment,
Which only bring pain and sorrow
For those whom you're holding, and their
sorrow becomes yours as well.

187

I am like a once overgrown field,
Now ploughed and seeded and nurtured for
new life.
Yet, alert to the dangers
From the crows of carelessness and the ego of
neglect.

188

I am like a flower,
Living in the sunless, brick cement lands of
indifference.
Ignored, not seen, an anomaly.
Yet, in drawing light and spreading light,
secret seeds are sown.

189

I am like a little bird,
You may not notice or know me.
I hop and scratch and do my stuff,
Yet, my song, if you listen, is about God.

190

I am like a butterfly,
In silence, I develop and emerge my form of
beauty,
Now drawing only nectar,
Now giving only love.

191

I am aware that my old attitudes and nature,
Weaken and deflect God's pure message,
Of introversion, love and true, pure action.
So holding this message, I must disappear.

192

I am in solitude,
Still, stable, beyond all influence.
A solitude beyond all vibrations and waves of
frenetic thought,
A solitude centred in the remembrance of
One.

193

I am like a post,
Believing I am free and light,
Yet, I am set and positioned from times past,
But still I can be used to stick things on.

194

I am the sum total of all my past thoughts and
actions
And my world and its furniture is the result of
these effects.
Now that I have stopped my anger and
despair and all my shouting at the universe,
I just have to ensure that my life is based on
truth.

195

I am in purdah,
I stay behind the veil of God's great love,
Hidden, in secret; protected,
Showing you only the third eye of knowledge.

196

I am not helping the poor and the suffering,
I am not helping my neighbour or the
deprived,
I am only helping the work of God,
Who is helping each and every soul.

197

I am here, but not here.
What you see is a form that holds my light,
I am in an awareness far beyond.
Look carefully and you too can find the way.

198

I am moving along according to my karma,
Carefully keeping things positive and right,
But I have not the strength to change,
So I must turn and take and draw God's
power.

199

I am listening and talking and reading,
Trying to grasp and understand,
Trying to assimilate life's great spiritual truths,
Yet, I am forgetting that it is only through
silence that realisation will come.

200

I am putting aside all business and concerns,
Now that God has come to meet his long-
estranged and separated family.
Yet, it is a world in denial, that is blind and
deaf,
So, I will help out to greet and to meet and
welcome Him with love.

201

I am a serial murderer,
As my inner voice, my godly conscious, calls
out "True!",
Yet, I turn away, ignore and kill its truth.
Is this the act of a compassionate soul?

202

I am the great deceiver.
Though knowing and accepting what is real
and true,
Yet, when I dance to other tunes,
You'll see on my face the mask of that
sorrow.

203

I am creating thoughts,
I am learning not to hold these thoughts,
I am creating thoughts just necessary for this
moment,
Then engaging the intellect, processing
significance.

204

I am awake and aware of your needs,
And I know if I doze or slip into sleep,
Your hands, which I hold, will fall away,
And you too will sleep and the darkness will
be complete.

205

I am sipping the nectar, the sweetness of
experience,
Yet, you still chew on old dried bread,
So why not let go of the books, the words, the
songs of the past,
And let silence take you into the love, heart
and happiness of the Spiritual Father.

206

I am the eyes through which the eyes of the
Father see,
And you're seeing into my eyes then can see
this One.
So I must clear and clean,
And keep my vision pure and true and
without desire.

207

I am allowing situations to resolve, things to
work out,
Standing back, not reacting, not interfering,
I allow things to settle and unravel,
By stepping in, I complicate and block the
healing.

208

I am learning to forgive.
By forgiving others, I become an example, a
teaching,
So there is no more to be said,
And, forgiving myself, I put down my stick.

209

I am in the company of the Father,
So why am I carrying a basket burden of
responsibilities?
Do I want the Father's role?
So throwing off this ill-fitting coat, I again
become the laughing, dancing child.

210

I am not upset that you reject my good
intentions,
Knowing this is the result of influence and
problems of past karma.
So I hold to my true intentions,
Knowing that they will eventually bring the
right result.

211

I am the way,
That only I can follow and that only I can
know,
And your way and your truth is only meant
for you.
So to hold this and be this, we certainly need
God's strength.

212

I am like a wheat field,
With seeds planted in seasons' past,
Now emerging and ripening,
But knowing it is only with patience and
through God's light that I will unfold.

213

I am remembering the souls of the world,
With thoughts of love and peace and hope,
And my thoughts then become their thoughts,
Enabling their truth and their path to open.

214

I am aware that my upheavals and difficulties,
Transfer and communicate the same,
And then others start to spin and twist and
tumble into fear,
Preventing stillness, experiences and ways
towards God.

215

I am like a garden,
Where everything is as it is, as it should be,
Natural, ordered, fragrant and peaceful,
And you are welcome to come and visit.

216

I am like a tree,
Full of what I have,
Just welcoming, accepting and sharing.
So is there anything more that you think I
should do?

217

I am like an empty box,
Whatever I receive it's from God,
So how can I keep it, hold it for myself,
So I keep filling, keep on giving and keep
nothing, like an empty box.

218

I am a figment of imagination,
An illusion of this present world,
And seeing me, you see what you think is also
you,
Not realising the wonder of your subtle, light
form.

219

I am not dependent or holding your hand,
For I know if you stumble, wander or fall,
I too, then, will do the same,
So I go my way, holding only God's steady
hand.

220

I am a flower in the flower field of the world,
Leaning, reaching for the Sun that draws and
holds my life,
Enabling me to experience my fragrance and
my beauty,
So I just have to keep open.

221

I am involved in a dance,
Where each dances to their own tune,
So no-one can know or dance with another,
So without the Lord of the Dance, all is chaos
and confusion.

222

I am aware at the time of need,
In the turmoil and break-up of the energetic
world,
Everyone will leave me, everything will fall
away,
Except the Father, who will carry me safely in
his eyes.

223

I am at times like the swaying branch,
Adjusting to the effects of circumstances and
influence,
But like the trunk, I am unshakable,
Held firm by the experience and power of the
triple seed state, of soul, drama and of God.

224

I am listening to your words of love,
To your wisdom, guidance and support,
Signposts, markers, clear lights for the
difficult days,
Yet also mirrors, enabling painless inner
change.

225

I am seeing the show and glamour of famous
souls,
Who attract and trap souls, the searching
moths,
Who being diverted from the meeting with
the One True Light,
Are then left only with the flickering shadows
and an empty heart.

226

I am in a most sacred place,
I have found the way long sought, long
hidden,
I have found the key, the door,
To the precious heart, the love heart, of the
Father.

227

I am reminding you of your greatness,
Of your virtues, specialities and power,
I remind you of the Father's tasks; making the
impossible possible,
So can't both of you get together to finish
your issues and last remaining defects?

228

I am trying to stay in the light,
Yet, through carelessness, I allow illusion's
shadow to cast its shade,
And so I stumble, misinterpret and experience
pain,
So please help and don't block my light.

229

I am like the golden grasses of the open field,
Open to the sky and the wind and the giving
sun,
At times, waving and whirling and bending or
just still,
So please don't criticise or judge or direct,
because that's what I'm doing.

230

I am sitting dazed and stunned and shaken,
For the house of my heart has been invaded
and broken into,
Everything has been swamped, flooded and
spoilt,
For the river of waste thought has found a
way in.

231

I am changing my attachments,
I am saying to God, "take all, it's yours.
Take the pain, the issues, the responsibilities,
the worries and problems."
I now feel great, but slightly uneasy, so I say
to God, "Ok, I'll help a little."

232

I am like a yacht,
Anchored in silence,
Held firm against the prevailing chaotic
currents,
Yet, waiting for the tide of the coming day.

233

I am experiencing the presence and support
of God,
In decisions, circumstances and relationships.
He is always with me,
So I need always to be with Him.

234

I am like a river lock,
Opening and then shutting off the past,
Filling to the necessary level,
So allowing the boat of my life to easily move
on.

ACKNOWLEDGEMENTS

Big thanks to
Lynn, Leza, Davina and of course Cy
For all your inspiration and support

Jim Ryan

Other Books by this author:

Meditation-The 13 Pathways to Happiness
In the Stillness
The Crystal Mind
How to Relax Your Mind
-The 10 Best Ways
(with Simon Ralph)

eternalpointoflight.com

Made in the USA
Charleston, SC
20 November 2016